Did You See What I Saw?

Poems about School

By Kay Winters
Illustrated by Martha Weston

PUFFIN BOOKS

PUFFIN BOOKS
Published by the Penguin Group
Penguin Putnam Books for Young Readers, 345 Hudson Street, New York, New York 10014, U.S.A.
Penguin Books Ltd, 27 Wrights Lane, London W8 5TZ, England
Penguin Books Australia Ltd, Ringwood, Victoria, Australia
Penguin Books Canada Ltd, 10 Alcorn Avenue, Toronto, Ontario, Canada M4V 3B2
Penguin Books (N.Z.) Ltd, 182-190 Wairau Road, Auckland 10, New Zealand

Penguin Books Ltd, Registered Offices: Harmondsworth, Middlesex, England

First published in the United States of America by Viking, a division of Penguin Books USA Inc., 1996
Published by Puffin Books, a division of Penguin Putnam Books for Young Readers, 2001

1 3 5 7 9 10 8 6 4 2

THE LIBRARY OF CONGRESS HAS CATALOGED THE VIKING EDITION AS FOLLOWS:
Winters, Kay.
Did you see what I saw? : poems about school / by Kay Winters ; illustrated by Martha Weston. p. cm.
Summary: Twenty-four poems about various aspects of going to school.
ISBN 0-670-87118-4
1. Children's poetry, American. 2. Schools—Juvenile poetry.
[1. American poetry. 2. Schools—Poetry.] I. Weston, Martha, ill. II. Title.
PS3573.I547D5 1996 811'.54—dc20 96-14696 CIP AC

"Runny Nose" first appeared in *Poetry Place Anthology*,
Instructor Books, Scholastic Inc.

Puffin Books ISBN 0-14-056265-6

Printed in the United States of America

For my mother, Luella Lanning,
who introduced me to poetry.

With special thanks to Deborah Brodie,
a gifted teacher and editor.
K.W.

This art is dedicated to Lissa,
who shouldn't be a bit surprised.
M.W.

School Bus

OUR BUS
is a
BIG
Bright
Loud
buMPY
STOP and start
Fast and s l o w
On and off
O p e n— shut
Yellow box
on wheels.
Stuffed with kids!

The Magic Box

I have squeaky new
back-to-school crayons,
lined up in a bright yellow box.
Each flavor has a pointy tip
and wears a paper jacket
just his size
waiting to be peeled off
his waxy back,
so he can make his mark.

Books Books Books

I LOVE TO READ!
Say those words.
Go those places.
See those sights.
Think those thoughts.
Meet those kids
who live in books,
waiting for me
To find them.

In the Circle

I love
to sit next
to my teacher.
She smells like flowers.
And she smiles at me
like I'm special.

Ooops!

I wrote a secret note.
Sent it three desks down
while the teacher
talked about
take-aways.

      SHE TOOK IT!

The Mistake

It's wrong.
So I erase
the space
where my mistake
showed its face.
Now a hole takes its place.

I think I'll climb in.

If I Were in Charge

Waiting in line,
a long thin line
takes time
every day
from our play.
We start
then we stop
while we

straighten our line
missing more time
on the way.

Why can't we bunch
as we go to our lunch?
Or walk in a group
for our soup?

There's a rule
in each school
about standing in line,
a stupid straight line.
I resign!

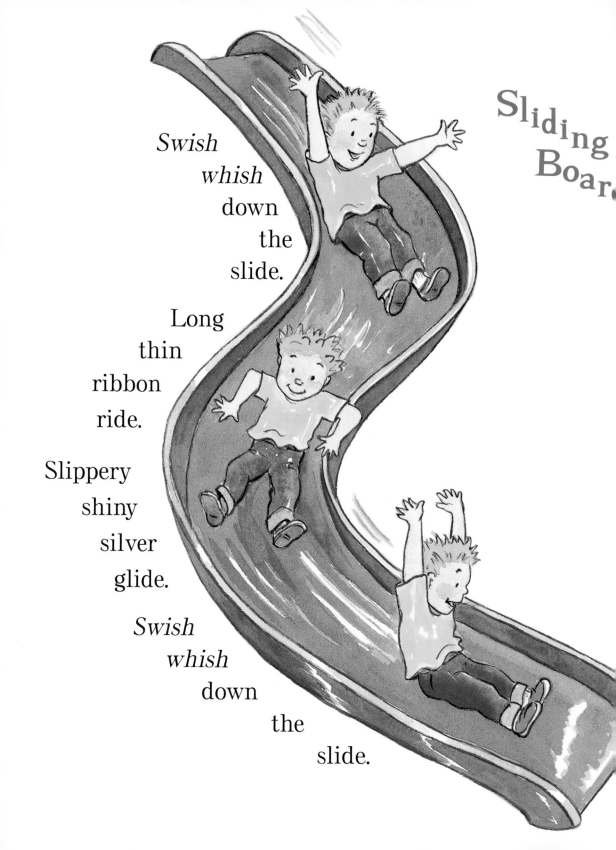

Swish
whish
down
the
slide.

Long
thin
ribbon
ride.

Slippery
shiny
silver
glide.

Swish
whish
down
the
slide.

Sliding
Board

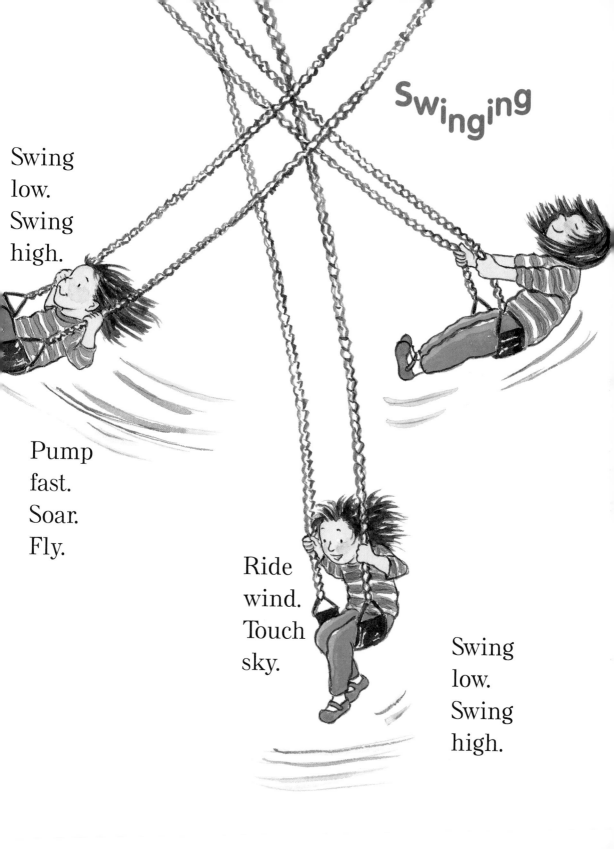

Swinging

Swing
low.
Swing
high.

Pump
fast.
Soar.
Fly.

Ride
wind.
Touch
sky.

Swing
low.
Swing
high.

Did You See What I Saw?

See saw
see saw.

He saw.
She saw.

She saw.
He saw.

I saw.
You saw.

We saw.
They saw.

See saw
SEE!

Not Fair

Why is it true?
When I know the answer
wave my hand wildly
and leap from my seat
she calls on you.

How can it be?
When I haven't a clue
roll my eyes skyward
and slump in my chair
she calls on me.

Lots of Spots

There's nothing shy about chicken pox.
Once they are here
they appear in flocks.

In the middle, up high, down low,
in places un-itchable
chicken pox grow.

They tickle.
They torture.
They tease you ... and then

They leave you
for Stephen.
And pop out again!

Runny Nose

It's just not funny
when your nose is runny.
You feel all soggy,
hoarse and froggy.
Your throat is scratching.
The germs are hatching.
You know it's catching.
Kerchoooooooooo!

Blizzard

No school!
A snow day!
Bet the teacher's really mad!
Today's the day we would have had
our math test.

Too bad!
How sad!
I'm glad!

Whoopee!

Groundhog Day

Did you ever wonder
if way down under,
in the tunnels and holes
groundhogs call home,
on February second,
they are calling a meeting?
Passing out name tags,
fixing the seating?
Counting the raised paws,
watching for cheating?
Deciding if winds
will use whisper or shout?
And also if recess
is inside or out.

The Valentine

It's a secret.
See?
I'm not
signing my name.

She can guess
all she wants
But she won't
guess me!

April Fool

It's the day
we play
tricks on the teacher.

It's the day
we put
tacks on her chair.

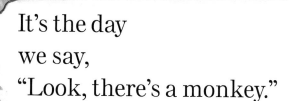

It's the day
we say,
"Look, there's a monkey."

And laugh when
she turns
and says, "Where?"

The Fountain

The drinking fountain
in the hall
is only for
the very tall.
I have to stand up on my toes.
The water squirts me in the nose.

We have a fountain
in first grade,
But truthfully,
I'd rather trade.
I *like* to drink out in the hall.
Someday I'll be VERY TALL.

The Class Pet

Yesterday
our turtle died.
We put him
in a box.

We covered him
with milkweed down,
and dug a hole
in the sandy ground.

Then we laid him
there alone
and marked his spot
with a shiny stone

and sang a good-bye song.

The Best

The best part
of the day
is when I hear
the teacher say,
"Sit by my chair
while I read."

We sprawl
on the rug.
It's like listening
to a hug,
while the story magic
pours over me.

Fun with Gum

I was only chewing
a little bit
on my pale pink
piece of gum.

Why did the teacher
throw such a fit?
What is so bad
about doing it?

I'm sitting here stewing.
I'm not even chewing.
She says with a shout,
"*Throw it out!*"

If I Could Vote

Reading would be repeated.
Handwriting deleted.
Artwork completed.
The playground heated.
Detention defeated.
Homework not needed!

Behind Closed Doors

When school is out
and the door is closed,
in the second grade room,
do you suppose ...
 the chalk talks?
 the floor snores?
 the clock knocks?
 the flag brags?
 the pencil stencils?
 the computer tutors?
 the numbers slumber?
 the books cook?
 the chairs pair?
 the fish wish?
 the flowers shower?

WHO KNOWS?

Saturday

It's my day.
A "hi!" day.

A run day.
A fun day.

A me day.
A see day.

A who day?
A you day.

A can't-wait-to-play day.
I-hope-you-can-stay day!